Seeing and Hearing

DAG HEWARD-MILLS

Parchment House

Unless otherwise stated, all Scripture quotations are taken from the King James Version of the Bible.

SEEING AND HEARING

Copyright © 2022 Dag Heward-Mills

First published by Parchment House 2022

Published by Parchment House 2022
1st Printing 2022

[77]Find out more about Dag Heward-Mills
Healing Jesus Campaign
Write to: evangelist@daghewardmills.org
Website: www.daghewardmills.org
Facebook: Dag Heward-Mills
Twitter: @EvangelistDag

ISBN: 978-1-64330-518-9

Contents

CHAPTER 1

Seeing and Hearing is Your Entrance into Wisdom

A wise man will HEAR, AND WILL INCREASE LEARNING; and a man of understanding shall attain unto wise counsels:

Proverbs 1:5

HEAR thou, my son, AND BE WISE, and guide thine heart in the way.

Proverbs 23:19

In this book, I want you to acquire the wisdom of seeing and hearing. I want you to become one of the wise sons who gives himself to the art of seeing and hearing.

A wise person will hear! It is only when you have acquired a certain wisdom in ministry that you give yourself to seeing and hearing. In order to serve God, people do all sorts of things. Some go to Bible school, some go to secular schools, some give offerings to men of God and some pray and fast. However, none of these activities compares with the important art of seeing and hearing.

Many of God's servants have not acquired the skill of seeing and hearing.

Seeing and hearing is the most important skill of a servant of God. Your wisdom is revealed in what you do. Wisdom is defined as the applying of your knowledge, your understanding, your experience and your common sense. Wisdom is how you apply what you know to your day-to-day life.

Seeing and hearing is the application of the knowledge you have received. You know that the Word is God and God is His Word. The more of the Word that enters you, the more of God you have in you! The more of God you have in you, the more anointed and powerful you are! Power belongs to God. Power is with God. The more you see the Word in action and the more you hear the Word, the more God comes into your life.

Seeing and hearing is the practical way to receive more of God into your life. That is why a wise man will hear and increase learning. That is why Scripture encourages a son to "hear and be wise".

Hearing is about listening to the preaching of God's word. It is about listening to the teachings that God has for you. The art of listening to preaching messages is one of the most important skills you can develop for yourself.

Seeing, on the other hand, involves having a live or living experience of ministry. Watching videos will help you in your quest of seeing and hearing. Watching someone do something has an effect on you. Watching someone set an example before you, is a message without words, telling you what you can do. It is also a message telling you what you should do and what you will do.

The art of seeing is the art of learning new things by watching. The art of seeing is the art of becoming experienced by observing! Surgeons learn how to operate by observing and assisting other surgeons. Seeing takes you further than hearing does. You cannot become a surgeon by hearing. Indeed, surgeons have attended many lectures. They have studied many things. But they cannot operate on anyone unless they have watched and observed and assisted many times. Would you like someone to operate on your heart, if he has just read a book about it?

There are many things you cannot appreciate until you see them. You cannot just hear about them! You cannot just hear of them! You must see them to know them well. And you must see them to understand them! You must see them so that you acquire the wisdom to do them.

Seeing and hearing is a practice of those who have a big ministry. Wise pastors give themselves to seeing and hearing. You need a lot of wisdom for ministry. Without wisdom, you cannot lead people. It is by wisdom that kings reign. It is by wisdom that princes lead with justice. Without wisdom you cannot build the church. Without wisdom you cannot construct the church buildings you will need.

The Bible says, "By wisdom a house is builded." (Proverbs 24:3). Without wisdom, you will never be promoted and you will never rise in ministry. Wisdom has wealth and riches in the left hand and long life in the right. *The art of seeing and hearing gives you access to this great wisdom that you need for ministry.*

Seeing and hearing is your God-given conduit of wisdom. It is a pipe from heaven through which fresh waters of wisdom will come to you. Make sure you are one of the ministers of God who is continuously listening to preaching and teaching.

Develop the art of seeing and hearing and become a wise man! Become wise for ministry! You are going to be wiser than your peers! You are going to be wiser than your teachers! You are going to be wiser than the elders!

Develop the art of listening to preaching messages over and over. Develop the art of listening to one message several times over. Develop the art of listening to a message until you can preach it yourself. Develop the art of listening to preaching and teaching until the message is part of you. Develop the art of listening to preaching until you can share the same message as though it is an original message.

CHAPTER 2

Seeing and Hearing
is Your Gift from God

The hearing ear, and the seeing eye, the Lord hath
made even both of them.

Proverbs 20:12

I see people who are so dull that they do not get stirred up by good preaching and teaching. They have not been given a hearing ear and a seeing eye. Those with this gift of seeing and hearing consider preaching and teaching to be a joyful sound. They are happy to receive podcasts, videos, teaching tapes, sound bites, audio notes and preaching messages.

When you have this gift, God opens your ear to hearing in a certain way. Some churches have the grace to hear, so their members are into listening to preaching messages. Hearing and seeing are not just abilities of those who have eyes and ears but are special spiritual abilities from God.

God gives you the grace to see and to hear. It is important to notice people who both see and hear. There are people who have been given the divine ability to hear but cannot see. There are others who can see but cannot hear.

Pray for the grace to see and hear. If you are not into seeing and hearing, you are not into ministry.

People who cannot physically see or hear cannot be taught anything at all. They cannot learn alphabets, they cannot count numbers, they cannot read and they cannot communicate. In the natural, the inability to see and hear is a serious handicap. That is why God seeks to give you the ability to see and to hear as a gift.

The grace to see and hear is evident when people teach and preach. You can always recognize a teacher who has been given a hearing ear and a seeing eye.

When you have been given a hearing ear and a seeing eye, preaching becomes a joyful sound. Those are the ones who know the joyful sound of preaching and teaching.

Blessed is the people that KNOW THE JOYFUL SOUND: they shall walk, O Lord, in the light of thy countenance.

Psalm 89:15

The sound of preaching and teaching coming out of a tape, a video, a podcast, the television, a phone or any other gadget is indeed a joyful sound for those who know what it means. When you have learnt to soak in messages from the word of God, you will discover a certain joy that others do not have.

My life has been changed by listening to preaching. The sound of preaching coming from my phone is indeed a joyful sound. As you read this book, the question is whether you have listened to preaching enough until it has become a joyful sound to you. Indeed, the ability to hear and see is God-given. It is God who enables you to see and to hear the Word that is preached.

If you do not listen to preaching and teaching you are handicapped. Receive this gift from God and lend yourself to seeing and hearing. Seeing and hearing is a big channel for God's blessings into your life. It is a channel of light, life, power and grace for you. Seeing and hearing is your channel for receiving wisdom. Become a pastor who is deep into watching videos, listening to preaching messages and soaking in teaching and the power of God.

CHAPTER 3

Seeing and Hearing Prevents You From Becoming Good for Nothing

TAKE THE GIRDLE that thou hast got, which is upon thy loins, and arise, go to Euphrates, and hide it there in a hole of the rock. So I went, and hid it by Euphrates, as the Lord commanded me. And it came to pass after many days, that the Lord said unto me, Arise, go to Euphrates, and take the girdle from thence, which I commanded thee to hide there. Then I went to Euphrates, and digged, and took the girdle from the place where I had hid it: and, behold, the girdle was marred, it was profitable for nothing. Then the word of the Lord came unto me, saying, Thus saith the Lord, After this manner will I mar the pride of Judah, and THE GREAT PRIDE OF JERUSALEM. THIS EVIL PEOPLE, WHICH REFUSE TO HEAR MY WORDS, WHICH WALK IN THE IMAGINATION OF THEIR HEART, AND WALK AFTER OTHER GODS, TO SERVE THEM, AND TO WORSHIP THEM, SHALL EVEN BE AS THIS GIRDLE, WHICH IS GOOD FOR NOTHING.
Jeremiah 13:4-10

The Girdle was Good for Nothing

The prophet Jeremiah was instructed to go and hide a girdle in a rock by the river. After many days, he was instructed to go and take the girdle. The girdle was destroyed and unusable. Then the word of the Lord was clear. The people who do not listen to the words of God become like this girdle: good for nothing!

The prophet Jeremiah declared that a person becomes good for nothing when he does not hear the word of God.

People who do not listen to preaching messages cannot be used by God. Have you wondered why God is not using you in a certain way? You are good for nothing when you do not give yourself to the art of seeing and hearing. Give yourself to preaching messages! Give yourself to soaking in camps, videos and preaching. The more you see and the more you hear, the more useful you are to God.

When you do not give yourself to seeing and hearing you become good for nothing. The scripture above shows us how the people became good for nothing because they would not hear God's words.

1. God describes those who do not hear His word as evil people.

2. God describes those who do not listen to messages as proud people.

3. God describes those who do not listen to messages as walking in the imagination of their hearts.

4. God describes those who do not listen to messages as idol worshippers.

5. God describes those who do not listen to messages as good for nothing.

Why is it that not listening to preaching and teaching has such a negative effect on your spirit? When you do not give yourself to seeing and hearing, you are exposed to a whole lot of evils. You hear other things! You hear conversations! You hear people chatting! You listen to the radio! You watch the news! All these do not build up your spirit. These things do not make you a mighty man of God.

If you only listen to a thirty-minute sermon on Sunday, you are not giving yourself to hearing the word of God. People watch television for hours. Many students have enough time to watch season one to season twenty-four of a television series. They have time enough to give their ears and their eyes to things created by wicked unbelievers. They soak in these dramas until they believe things that they should not believe and receive spirits that they should not receive.

Of course, such people will be good for nothing in the ministry! It is time to give yourself to seeing and hearing the word of God constantly. Soak in the word of God for hours! Listen to the same teaching several times over! Listen to the word of God until it becomes a joyful sound!

You are good for nothing in the ministry when you do not give yourself to seeing and hearing!

CHAPTER 4

Seeing and Hearing Guarantees You A Channel for Receiving

Be watchful, and strengthen the things which remain, that are ready to die: for I have not found thy works perfect before God. REMEMBER THEREFORE HOW THOU HAST RECEIVED AND HEARD, and hold fast, and repent. If therefore thou shalt not watch, I will come on thee as a thief, and thou shalt not know what hour I will come upon thee.

Revelation 3:2-3

Remember how you have received and heard! I can remember how I have received and heard. I remember when I was a medical student, I was listening to preaching by Kenneth Hagin. I heard a voice clearly and I received the power of God on my life - I heard and received the anointing of God on my life. Anyone who has received from God can remember how he has heard and received!

Seeing and hearing is the avenue for receiving something from God. The scripture above tells us to remember how we have received something from God. Look around you and notice the people who do not spend hours soaking in messages, camps, songs, teachings and powerful preaching. You will see that they have not received much.

You will notice how dry some preachers are. It is because they have not been listening to preaching.

Those who do not hear do not receive impartations of the anointing. You will not receive impartations unless you are into seeing and hearing!

Those who do not hear do not receive inflows of wisdom. You will not receive any wisdom unless you are into seeing and hearing!

Those who do not hear do not receive inflows of counsel. You will not receive knowledge unless you are into seeing and hearing!

Those who do not hear do not receive the grace of God. You will not receive grace unless you are into seeing and hearing!

Those who do not hear do not receive inflows of divine guidance. You will not receive direction unless you are into seeing and hearing!

Those who do not hear do not receive inflows of faith. Faith comes by hearing!

Those who do not hear do not receive the power of God. You will not receive any power unless you are into seeing and hearing.

Those who do not hear do not receive inflows of the Word. You will not receive anything unless you are into seeing and hearing.

Those who do not hear do not receive revelation. You will not receive any revelation unless you are into seeing and hearing.

Those who do not hear do not receive insight. You will not receive any insight unless you are into seeing and hearing.

CHAPTER 5

Seeing and Hearing Gives Life to Your Ministry

Therefore speak I to them in parables: because they seeing see not; and hearing they hear not, neither do they understand. And in them is fulfilled the prophecy of Esaias, which saith, By hearing ye shall hear, and shall not understand; and seeing ye shall see, and shall not perceive: FOR THIS PEOPLE'S HEART IS WAXED GROSS, AND THEIR EARS ARE DULL OF HEARING, AND THEIR EYES THEY HAVE CLOSED; lest at any time they should see with their eyes, and hear with their ears, and should understand with their heart, and should be converted, and I should heal them.

Matthew 13:13-15

Dullness of hearing is dullness of ministry! A dead body has its eyes and ears closed up! Nothing enters! The dead body sees nothing, feels nothing and hears nothing. When people are dull of hearing and their eyes have closed, they are dead as far as ministry is concerned. Many people experience deadness in ministry. A terrible and profound deadness descends on those who are unable to hear preaching. Indeed, a sign that deadness has descended on you in ministry is when you are unable to listen to important preaching messages.

I have visited many churches. I have seen many pastors who look dull, uninterested and unresponsive. It is very difficult for these expressionless pastors to learn anything new. They can hardly open their eyes to look at the title of a book. They are past learning. They cannot receive! They feel sleepy within the first few minutes of a sermon.

Of whom we have many things to say, and hard to be uttered, SEEING YE ARE DULL OF HEARING. For when for the time ye ought to be teachers, ye have need that one teach you again which be the first principles of the oracles of God; and are become such as have need of milk, and not of strong meat.

Hebrews 5:11-12

A person who is dull of hearing cannot be a successful teacher of the Word. You must learn to overcome dullness of hearing. Remember that dullness of hearing means dullness of ministry! You must also decide never to have your eyes closed.

What does it mean to be dull of hearing? To be dull of hearing is to be tired of listening to preaching. The messages no longer excite you! The preaching no longer provokes you! When you are dull of hearing, you have reached a critical point in your ministry. If you want to go forward, you need to become excited again about hearing. One of the ways to fight dullness of hearing is to keep searching for messages and things to listen to. I promise you; life is going to come into your ministry when you listen to a message with your eyes and ears open.

One night, as I was listening to a preaching message whilst I was praying, I received a powerful impartation from the Lord. I jumped out of my couch and began to pace up and down in my study. Nothing could put me back in the chair. I was more awake at 2.00 am than I would be at midday. I had heard something so amazing that it had refocused my life. Because my ears were open, I received life.

The deadness was gone! The sleepiness was gone! The slumber was gone! So much power had come into me because of what I had heard. I do not remember what I was praying about but I remember what I heard. Indeed, that one night of listening to preaching changed my whole life.

God is speaking to pastors who are dead and blind. God is speaking to those who are in ministry but cannot watch videos of anointed men preaching. What are you doing watching movies but not watching anointed preaching? Who is blind but my servant? Many servants of God are blind. They simply do not see the videos that are important for them. You will never become what God wants you to become unless you watch certain videos.

Hear, ye deaf; and look, ye blind, that ye may see. WHO IS BLIND, BUT MY SERVANT? OR DEAF, AS MY MESSENGER that I sent? Who is blind as he that is perfect, and blind as the Lord's servant? Seeing many things, but thou observest not; opening the ears, but he heareth not.

Isaiah 42:18-20

Who is deaf as the messenger of God? Messengers of God are not supposed to be deaf. Messengers of God are supposed to be hearing and hearing and hearing! Rise up today and expose yourself to important preaching that God has for you. Get the messages that are essential for your ministry. Line them up! Start tasting them! Start sampling them and locate the one that excites your spirit. Do not be a deaf messenger of God.

One day, I visited a pastor who had become extremely dull in the ministry. He was so dull and dead that his church was nearly empty. I made a point of finding out if he was listening to any preaching at all. I found out that he had not listened to any preaching for almost a year. No wonder a great deadness had descended on his ministry! He had almost no members in his church.

This pastor held a special programme but because his ministry was dead, dull and dying, he had to go into the neighbourhood to gather any children he could find to make up the congregation. He gathered these children because the visiting preacher would have been speaking to empty classroom chairs. Deadness and dullness descend upon those who do not give themselves to seeing and hearing.

CHAPTER 6

Seeing and Hearing Guarantees Divine Direction

Behold, the days come, saith the Lord God, THAT I WILL SEND A FAMINE IN THE LAND, NOT A FAMINE OF BREAD, NOR A THIRST FOR WATER, BUT OF HEARING THE WORDS OF THE LORD: And THEY SHALL WANDER FROM SEA TO SEA, and from the north even to the east, they shall run to and fro to seek the word of the Lord, and shall not find it. In that day shall the fair virgins and young men faint for thirst.

Amos 8:11-13

When there is a famine of hearing the words of God, you are left to wander around from sea to sea!

Seeing and hearing is your key to divine guidance. In the ministry, you will need minute-by-minute guidance from the Holy Spirit. You cannot do well in ministry without divine guidance. We are the sheep of His hand. Sheep need to be led and brought to green pastures.

Sheep are the animals that are most dependent on human beings. That shows how dependent we are on divine guidance. What hope does a sheep have, if it is walking from Accra to Lagos by itself? What hope does a sheep have, if it is taking a journey by itself from Johannesburg to Nairobi? Do you think it will get there? I don't!

When you listen to preaching messages, you will receive guidance for your ministry. I can remember occasions when I received guidance for my ministry as I listened to preaching. One night, when I was twenty-five years old, I was listening to a message by Kenneth Hagin and I heard a voice that said, "From today you can teach." This experience changed my whole life. From that time, I knew that I should teach the word of God. I knew that I should emphasize on teaching the word of God.

On another occasion, I was listening to another teacher of the word of God. I sat up all night in a chair, praying and listening to this great man of God. I fell asleep and woke up in the middle of the night. When I woke up, I heard him speaking about an evil spirit that he had identified in America. It was so strange to hear this man identify this problem and share it on the message. Although this man of God was dead, God was speaking to me and giving me guidance on what I should do in my life and ministry. I knew that I was dealing with the same evil power that he was describing. I knew who my enemy was. I received guidance for my ministry.

When I became a pastor, I did not know how to preach or what to preach about. I would listen to Fred Price teaching and preaching in his church. As I listened to his preaching, I learnt about topics that I could also preach about. I learnt how to title my messages by listening to his messages. I learnt how to preach with points by listening to him preaching. I learnt how to preach a series of messages, week after week by listening to him. One day I heard him preaching on the topic, "Six Principles to Obtain Strong Faith." I was so intrigued by the topic. I developed my own series called, "Seven Great Principles." God was guiding me and teaching me on how to be a pastor and how to teach my flock.

Although God had called me, I needed guidance on how to proceed, on how to teach, on what to teach and what to do. I received all these through listening to preaching. When there is a famine of hearing the words of God, you are left to wander around from sea to sea.

CHAPTER 7

Seeing and Hearing Improves Prayer

He that TURNETH AWAY HIS EAR FROM HEARING the law, EVEN HIS PRAYER shall be abomination.

Proverbs 28:9

Do not allow your prayer life to become an abomination by turning your ears away from hearing! A prayer life that is an abomination is a prayer life that is disgusting and useless. You should not allow your prayers to become disgusting and useless. Even your prayer is affected by hearing. Turning your ear away from listening to preaching will affect you in countless ways, including prayer.

It is not easy to sit in a quiet room and pray for four continuous hours. Have you wondered why there is nothing like four continuous hours of prayer in your life? Those who do not hear the Word cannot pray properly. Hearing greatly affects prayer.

It is very difficult to pray by the sea because the sounds of the waves take away the sound of your prayer. You do not hear anything and it is very difficult to continue speaking to the sound of the waves. That is why those who listen to preaching and music whilst praying have great prayer lives and those who do not, have abominable prayer lives.

The worst thing you can do to yourself is to stop hearing. Once you stop hearing you are in the worst possible state of your spiritual life. Even your prayer life is affected when you stop listening to preaching.

It is necessary to listen to good Christian music whilst you pray. One day, a brother gave me a collection of long-play Christian reggae music. This music collection played continually for five hours. Whenever I put on this music, I was rolling for five non-stop hours of prayer. Hearing greatly affects your ability to stay awake and pray.

Prayer is an art. Prayer is the ability to stay awake in the night. Prayer is the ability to stay alive and to communicate to God who does not utter a word in response to your many words. Prayer is the ability to keep on talking to God about different topics without useless repetition. Prayer is the ability to talk sensibly to the most important person in the universe.

How do you think God feels when you keep falling asleep in front of Him? Would you fall asleep in front of the Queen of England? Why do you not develop the art of seeing and hearing so that you can be a powerful prayer warrior? Seeing and hearing is a master key to spirituality and to effectiveness in prayer.

One day, I learnt the lesson of seeing and hearing with prayer the hard way. I checked into a hotel in a European city to wait on God. It was a terrible time because there was no sound in the room. The only source of seeing and hearing was the television that was loaded with horrible, polluted stuff. It was the usual news and the usual perverted movies. I could hardly pray in this cold, hard and silent environment. From that time, I never allowed myself to be anywhere without the ability to create an atmosphere where I can see and hear from God.

God is showing you today, the importance of developing the art of seeing and hearing whilst praying. I cannot imagine going to pray somewhere without having all my preaching messages and all my music. How long will my prayers last if I do not allow powerful anointed videos to play whilst I am praying? When that powerful anointed video is playing, it is as though you are part of a miracle service during your prayer time. On countless occasions I have enjoyed the power of God as I spent hours in prayer with a video playing.

CHAPTER 8

Seeing and Hearing Guarantees Flexibility

Yet the Lord testified against Israel, and against Judah, by all the prophets, and by all the seers, saying, TURN YE FROM YOUR EVIL WAYS, and keep my commandments and my statutes, according to all the law which I commanded your fathers, and which I sent to you by my servants the prophets. NOTWITHSTANDING THEY WOULD NOT HEAR, BUT HARDENED THEIR NECKS, LIKE TO THE NECK OF THEIR FATHERS, THAT DID NOT BELIEVE IN THE LORD THEIR GOD.

2 Kings 17:13-14

Hear my words! Do not harden your neck! This is the command of the Lord. People who do not hear the word of the Lord are hardened and stubborn. Turn from your ways of not listening to preaching and watching preaching. It is an evil thing when you are no longer soft enough to hear from the Lord. God is angry with you because you will not hear His word. Incline your ears! Make yourself available. Spend some money to acquire all the preaching that you need so that you can watch, listen and learn.

Show me how much you listen to preaching and watch videos and I will tell you how soft and flexible you are in the hands of God.

People who do not listen to preaching are hardened, stiffened ministers. Through my travels, I have met many hardened ministers who can no longer be taught anything. They are hardened and set in their ways. God can do very little with hardened people. When you quietly listen to preaching and teaching, you will receive faith for flexibility in your ministry and faith to be humble.

A person with a hearing ear is a softened personality. Children listen when a grown-up speaks. They listen with rapt attention, believing most of what is said. Listening and hearing is indeed a sign of the softness of a child.

Why would you be listening to a message if you were not soft enough to learn something? Why would you be watching a video if you were not soft enough to receive guidance for radical changes? The very fact that you are watching that video shows that you are seeking for something that will change you and help you in your walk with God.

A hearing ear is the ear of a soft person: someone who is pliable in the hands of God. If you are into seeing and hearing, you are delivered from hardness and stubbornness. All forms of stubbornness and hardness reveal the inability to hear. When a person is stubborn you will have long meetings with the person but the point will not be understood.

Let this be a sign to you: seeing and hearing is a sign of how soft and flexible you are in the hands of God. Inflexibility is your way to disaster! A hardened neck is a very bad thing. It calls for destruction.

He, that being often reproved hardeneth his neck, shall suddenly be destroyed, and that without remedy.

Proverbs 29:1

The more you listen to preaching and teaching, the more you prove that you do not have a hardened and stiffened neck.

CHAPTER 9

Seeing and Hearing Guarantees a Rise to the Next Level

So then faith cometh by hearing, and hearing by the word of God.

Romans 10:17

Perhaps this is the most important scripture when it comes to the art of seeing and hearing. The main thing you get from hearing is faith. Through hearing, your faith jumps up to the next level. Without faith you cannot please God. Without faith you cannot enter the ministry.

Perhaps, you are already in the ministry. Through hearing and through faith, you will jump up to the next level of ministry.

You cannot have faith for different aspects of ministry until you learn to hear about them. When you do, you receive faith for the different aspects of God and ministry and you begin to operate there. Through hearing, you will receive faith for the next level of ministry.

For every level of ministry I entered, I did so through faith that came from hearing. When I was in secondary school, I would listen to preaching by Kenneth Hagin. He spoke of the call of God. He spoke about Jesus. When I heard him speaking about Jesus, I believed that Jesus Christ was real.

He described how Jesus walked into his room and spoke with him. I was enthralled and captivated with these visions. The thought that Jesus Christ was a real person who was watching us, listening to us and communicating with us, completely fascinated me.

I could not get over the fact that Jesus Christ was a real person. Jesus was real! My faith to be in the ministry was greatly increased. I received faith to enter the ministry by listening to preaching.

I received faith for writing books and producing tapes by listening to Kenneth Hagin. I heard him describe how the Lord appeared to him and told him what to do with his tape ministry. I heard him describe how an angel appeared to him and how he received the finances to do his tapes ministry.

I heard him tell how Jesus warned him not to engage two gentlemen who wanted to run his tapes ministry. I heard him describe how Jesus told him to put his preaching into the printed page.

Most definitely, all these messages affected my life. They made me believe in the ministry. They made me believe in Jesus, in angels and in supernatural guidance. Many of the things that I do in the ministry today are related to the things that I heard Kenneth Hagin speak about.

When I was growing up, I thought that marriage was a negative thing. I considered it to be a trap of considerable proportions. However, as I listened to Fred Price preach about marriage, I changed my mind and developed faith for marriage. I entered marriage with great faith and great hopes which I had received from preaching. Your faith for marriage will rise when you listen to certain kinds of preaching.

Every level of your life is determined by the faith you have. Without faith you cannot go to the next level. Faith for the next level comes by hearing.

One day, I listened to preaching by Kenneth Hagin on the miracles of Jesus. I listened to him analyse and teach about every single miracle of Jesus. I was greatly impacted by those series of messages. I saw each and every miracle of Jesus as a special event that was teaching us something. I understood the power of God and accepted the mystery of miraculous ministry as I listened to Kenneth Hagin teaching on this amazing subject. If you listen to preaching that makes fun of healing and miracles you will not develop faith for it and you will not rise into that level of ministry. Seeing and hearing is the master key to your next level of ministry.

I never used to understand why people would fall down under the power of God. I felt most of them were faking it. One day, I listened to preaching by Kenneth Hagin on why people fall under the power. He gave many powerful examples from the word of God of this amazing phenomenon. I received faith for that level of ministry. What level of ministry do you desire to rise into? You need to have faith for that.

I met a young man who had grown up in a pastor's house where the husband was always fighting with his wife. Because of this scenario, he found Christianity hypocritical and he hated the church. He wanted to be as far from ministry as possible. One day, this young man encountered some preaching messages and he listened to them for four years. After four years of listening to these messages, he felt a great positivity towards ministry. All the negativity was gone. Faith had come into him and he now had power to enter the ministry. He said, "I want to serve God. I want to preach. I want to minister." All these were feelings that he had never had before.

People remain at a low level of life and ministry because they have set aside the art of seeing and hearing. Seeing and hearing is your channel to receive faith for the next level. You will climb into ministry as you hear good and positive things about the ministry.

One day, a minister I know locked himself up in a house for twenty-one days. For twenty-one days he fasted and prayed and listened to Kenneth Hagin tapes. When he came out of this fast, he had become a faith teacher and he drew crowds of people to himself. In no time he had a mega church. He came out of nowhere and turned into a Christian celebrity almost overnight. Such is the power of seeing and hearing!

There was a servant of a man of God who had no education. He could not even write his name. He had no education at all. To everyone's shock, this man of God died suddenly, leaving behind a disconsolate widow and a surprised church. The man of God's servant however, took the tapes of his master and decided to soak them in. He would be found on mountaintops, walking around, fasting with earphones in his ears, soaking in the messages of his dead master. This servant, who gave himself to the art of seeing and hearing, turned into a great man of God and had a worldwide ministry too.

Great faith comes into you as you give yourself to listening. The art of seeing and hearing is your master key to a higher level of life and ministry.

CHAPTER 10

Seeing and Hearing Guarantees Humility

HEAR YE, AND GIVE EAR; BE NOT PROUD: for the Lord hath spoken. Give glory to the Lord your God, before he cause darkness, and before your feet stumble upon the dark mountains, and, while ye look for light, he turn it into the shadow of death, and make it gross darkness. BUT IF YE WILL NOT HEAR IT, MY SOUL SHALL WEEP IN SECRET PLACES FOR YOUR PRIDE; and mine eye shall weep sore, and run down with tears, because the Lord's flock is carried away captive. Say unto the king and to the queen, humble yourselves, sit down: for your principalities shall come down, even the crown of your glory.

Jeremiah 13:15-18

When people are proud, they no longer hear nor receive. Think about it! A child will sit down humbly and listen to all that you have to tell him. As the child grows older and older, his pride also grows bigger and he no longer wants to hear what the parent has to say.

One day, a child said to his father, "I have obeyed you all these years and done what you wanted me to do. Now, I want to do what I want to do. I hated following your instructions all these years. I want to do what I want to do." Only pride makes a person speak in this way. It is only when you are proud that you do not want to hear what your father has to say on a given topic. It is only when you are proud that you no longer incline your ears to what your father has to say.

Over the years I noticed how several of my pastors stopped listening to my messages. They stopped soaking in the messages. They seemed aloof and did not see the need to soak in the messages.

The scripture says clearly, "Hear ye and give ear! Be not proud!" In other words, pride is the reason why people stop listening to preaching. When you do not have time to listen to the preaching of the Word, the Lord's flock is carried away captive. The congregation is affected by your failure to soak in preaching and teaching properly.

When people are small in their own eyes, they will listen to preaching and soak it in. When they are big in their eyes they say, "Do we have to listen to this preaching? Is it really necessary? Can we not study the Bible for ourselves? What about those who do not have all these electronic gadgets to listen to preaching?" They say things like, "He is trying to turn us into clones of himself. Can we not study the Bible ourselves?"

However, the apostle Paul told Timothy what exactly to preach. Paul said;

Thou therefore, my son, be strong in the grace that is in Christ Jesus. And the things that thou hast heard

**of me among many witnesses, the same commit thou
to faithful men, who shall be able to teach others also.**

2 Timothy 2:1-2

Paul said to Timothy, "Do you remember the things you heard from me? Just preach the same things!" *Timothy's ability to preach was dependent on his ability to hear.* This is the reason why deafness goes with dumbness. Most deaf people are also dumb. They cannot speak because they cannot hear. Paul was telling Timothy to keep hearing so that he could keep preaching.

Are you soaking in preaching messages? Do you have time to lie on the floor and spend hours in the presence of God? One day, I found about eighty-five messages on a particular topic, preached by a man of God whom I admired. I started listening to this series from the first message. I listened to all the eighty-five messages. Then I listened to them over and over again. As the weeks and months passed by, I noticed an upgrade in the anointing that was on my life.

It is your pride that tells you that all the messages are the same. "Oh, I know what this message is about." That is what people say. But you know nothing! When they look at preaching messages they say, "It's all the same thing."

When I was listening to those eighty-five messages, I could have said they were all the same. But every message is unique, even when the titles are similar. You may hear some casual side comments in a message that will change your whole life.

The seed that was intentionally planted may have no effect in your life; but the seeds that fell by the roadside may be the ones to actually bear fruit. You may be surprised at the effects of the roadside seeds that enter your heart when you are listening to preaching.

One day, I was listening to a message by Kenneth Hagin. He was talking about the ministry of a prophet. He shared about how a prophet sees and knows things. He explained how he visited a church and the pastor tried to cheat him out of his agreed honorarium. Then he made a comment that was actually a side comment. He said, "In the ministry, it is important to bend over backwards to be honest." That statement stayed with me as I grew up in the ministry. "Bend over backwards to be honest."

Over the years I have watched how people in the ministry lie and pretend so much, thereby destroying themselves. They do not realise how destructive dishonesty is. Your whole life and ministry can change when it is discovered that you are telling lies or pretending. Hearing a side comment on honesty can change your life. I heard that for myself many years ago when I was listening to a message and it changed my life.

CHAPTER 11

Seeing and Hearing is the Father's business

AND IT CAME TO PASS, THAT AFTER THREE DAYS THEY FOUND HIM IN THE TEMPLE, SITTING IN THE MIDST OF THE DOCTORS, BOTH HEARING THEM, AND ASKING THEM QUESTIONS. And all that heard him were astonished at his understanding and answers. And when they saw him, they were amazed: and his mother said unto him, Son, why hast thou thus dealt with us? behold, thy father and I have sought thee sorrowing. And he said unto them, how is it that ye sought me? WIST YE NOT THAT I MUST BE ABOUT MY Father's business?

Luke 2:46-49

T his passage is not teaching that hearing the Word will help you to do the Father's business. This passage is teaching us that hearing *is* the Father's business. Jesus was about His Father's business! His Father's business was to listen to preaching and to ask questions about it.

Jesus could not be found by His parents. He was lost in the temple. They found him after three days. His parents were amazed when they found Him. "What are you doing here?" What was Jesus doing there? He was busy hearing the doctors of the temple share the Word. All that Jesus wanted to do was to hear the Word. Jesus said to His parents, "Don't you know that I must be about My Father's business?"

Jesus Christ was found doing His Father's business. Jesus Christ was not winning souls. Jesus Christ was not praying. Jesus Christ was not fasting. Jesus Christ was not a volunteer cleaner in the temple. Jesus Christ was not ushering visitors in and out of the temple. Jesus Christ was not collecting offering or counting the offering. Jesus Christ was not a security officer at the temple. So what exactly did He mean when He said He was about His Father's business?

Jesus Christ was hearing the word of God and asking questions. That is the Father's business! Do you want to be about the Heavenly Father's business? Then get down to listening the word of God. Why was Jesus asking questions? Jesus was asking questions to stir up the doctors of the law to speak even more. He wanted them to speak endlessly so that He could learn as much as He could.

Pastors who do not spend time listening, seeing and hearing are far away from the Father's business. Being in full time ministry affords you the opportunity to give yourself wholly to seeing the ministry in action and hearing all the messages that you need to hear.

Till I come, give attendance to reading, to exhortation, to doctrine. Neglect not the gift that is in thee, which was given thee by prophecy, with the laying on of the hands of the presbytery. Meditate upon these things;

give thyself wholly to them; that thy profiting may appear to all. Take heed unto thyself, and unto the doctrine; continue in them: for in doing this thou shalt both save thyself, and them that hear thee.

1 Timothy 4:13-16

You will notice that Paul advised Timothy to give himself wholly to the ministry. Why was he to give himself wholly to the ministry? What would he be doing when he gave himself wholly to ministry? He would be giving himself to reading, to exhortation, to doctrine and to meditation of the Word. That is what it means to give yourself wholly. To be in the ministry is to invest in yourself!

Paul said, "Take heed to yourself." Soak in the Word for yourself. Build up your faith for yourself. Invest in your own spirit. This is exactly what is expected of you in full time ministry. Jesus knew that He had to soak in the Word if He had to fulfil God's calling and commission.

How come so few ministers of God know this principle of hearing the Word? How come so few ministers actually listen to audio messages? Ministers sit there looking old, worn out and expressionless. They cannot stay awake for even fifteen minutes. They start yawning in the first three minutes of every preaching, no matter how exciting it is.

How come you are not hunting for storehouses of good preaching that change lives? There is so much out there that can lift you up. There are so many podcasts and messages on the internet that would change your ministry and your level. If you would only bother to listen to the messages God brings to you, you would begin your journey into the Father's business.

What are you doing in town? Why are you always walking around and sweating so much? It is time to give yourself to meditation, reading and listening to the Word. Seeing and hearing is your master key to the Father's business! Seeing and hearing will open you up to new dimensions of your Father's business.

CHAPTER 12

Seeing and Hearing Engineers a Great Change

AND HE FELL TO THE EARTH, AND HEARD A VOICE SAYING UNTO HIM, SAUL, SAUL, WHY PERSECUTEST THOU ME? And he said, who art thou, Lord? And the Lord said, I am Jesus whom thou persecutest: it is hard for thee to kick against the pricks. And he trembling and astonished said, Lord, what wilt thou have me to do? And the Lord said unto him, Arise, and go into the city, and it shall be told thee what thou must do. And the men which journeyed with him stood speechless, hearing a voice, but seeing no man. And Saul arose from the earth; and when his eyes were opened, he saw no man: but they led him by the hand, and brought him into Damascus.

Acts 9:4-8

Hearing a Word from the Lord can bring about a great change in your life and ministry. Saul heard one statement, "Saul, Saul, why persecutest thou me?" This message was enough to change his whole life.

Through hearing, you will receive faith to make a great change in your life and ministry. Great change is made possible when you hear certain things.

The gospel of Jesus Christ is the word of God. It is so powerful in its ability to heal and to change people. One day, a man of God attended my crusade. He was amazed at the numbers of people who attended that crusade. He blurted out, "Only the gospel of Jesus Christ can gather such a crowd." This man of God was used to preaching to large congregations all over the world. But the crowd that had assembled at the field was far more than anything he had ever seen. That night he saw, at first-hand, the power of the gospel. The gospel is a specific kind of message that is able to change the lives of people. It is good news to the lost soul.

One day, a lady got married to a drug-dealing young man. Soon, she was deep into the drugs lifestyle like her husband. But one day something happened. She was driving along the road when she heard Billy Graham preaching the gospel. She said, she remembered clearly what he said. His message was simple: "God commended His love towards us that while we were yet sinners Christ died for us."

She parked by the side of the road and gave her life to Jesus Christ.

Her salvation was real and complete. She began to intercede for her husband who later was converted and even became a pastor.

Do not assume that others know what you know. They need to hear the Word just as you heard it. When Paul heard those words, "Saul, Saul, why persecutest thou me?" a great change was released into his life.

Hearing and seeing bring about a great change. When you hear the word of God, something wonderful happens; great changes are engineered in your soul. The Word may be short. It may be brief! It may be a few words! But one word from God is all you need. Please open yourself up to the art of seeing and hearing. You will be amazed at the great change that will come into your life and ministry. Years ago, a man shared with me the reason why Jesus died for me. He said, "Without the shedding of blood there is no remission of sins." That statement brought about a great change in my life. I am saved today and washed by the blood of Jesus because those words that I heard were powerful words. Please open yourself up to the art of seeing and hearing. You are about to hear something that is life-changing. Great changes will occur and everyone will acknowledge that God spoke to you.

CHAPTER 13

Seeing and Hearing Guarantees Your Relationship with the Holy Spirit

THIS ONLY WOULD I LEARN OF YOU, RECEIVED YE THE SPIRIT BY THE WORKS OF THE LAW, OR BY THE HEARING OF FAITH? ... He therefore that ministereth to you the Spirit, and worketh miracles among you, doeth he it by the works of the law, or by the hearing of faith?

Galatians 3:2, 5

Seeing and hearing will open you up to the Holy Spirit. Seeing and hearing will open you up to the anointing. Hearing with faith will enable you to receive the Holy Spirit. Hearing with faith will also enable you to minister the Holy Spirit.

Do you not want to receive the anointing of the Holy Spirit to change everything about your life and ministry? Without faith you cannot relate with the Holy Spirit. You must believe in the existence of the Holy Spirit. The more you hear about the Holy Spirit, the more you can receive the anointing. The Spirit is received by hearing with faith.

Peter went to Cornelius' house and preached to the household. As they listened, their faith was stirred up and they received the Holy Spirit. Indeed, the Holy Spirit fell on the people as Peter preached.

While Peter yet spake these words, the Holy Ghost fell on all them which heard the word.

Acts 10:44

As Peter preached, the people had faith and they were able to receive the Spirit. As you listen to the word of God, your belief in the mighty Holy Spirit will increase. And you will receive unspeakable gifts that you had only imagined beforehand.

The first time I heard preaching about the Holy Spirit I did not understand it. Benny Hinn was preaching about "Good morning, Holy Spirit." It was too mystical and spooky for me. I could not relate with it at all. I simply rejected it because I could not relate with it.

However, as I kept listening and watching Benny Hinn's video, my heart softened and I began to listen more intently and watch more closely. It is important to listen more than once. Indeed, it is important to listen several times to the same message.

The reality of the Holy Spirit was completely foreign to me. As I soaked in the Word several times, I began to admire the ministry of the Holy Spirit.

The more I listened and watched Benny Hinn speak about the anointing, the more I liked it. You receive the Spirit by the hearing of faith.

One day, I found twelve messages on the anointing. These twelve messages became my daily bread and butter. I realised how much I had changed. Some years before, I would not have been able to relate with such messages. But through the art of seeing and hearing, I was receiving the Holy Spirit.

You can also become a hearer of such things. You have to take a series of messages on an important topic for your life. Soak them in until you are saturated. Keep listening to things you do not understand. You will suddenly begin to understand them. Hearing with faith makes you receive the anointing.

I listened to Kenneth Hagin for ten years before I received the anointing to teach. One night, whilst praying, I put on a tape recorder to play all night. At about 2.00am, something jumped out of the tape and entered into my belly.

I felt something slip deep into my belly and I heard a voice saying, "From today you can teach." I had received the Spirit by the hearing of faith! I was anointed!

You too can be anointed. You can receive the Holy Spirit by faith. Paul told us how to receive the Holy Spirit. He asked, "Received ye the Holy Spirit by the works of the law or by the hearing of faith?" (Galatians 3:2).

Ministering the Spirit is different from receiving the Spirit. You must be able to minister the Spirit to people. You must be able to pray for people to receive the baptism of the Holy Spirit. You must be able to pray for people and experience strong manifestations of the power of the Holy Spirit. Such things cannot happen unless you hear with faith. Keep listening!

CHAPTER 14

"Hearing Twice"

God hath spoken once; twice have I heard this; that power belongeth unto God.

Psalm 62:11

66 Hearing twice" is the art of listening repetitively. "Hearing twice" is the art of listening to preaching several times over.

It is only when you listen to a message twice that you actually hear from God.

Repeated hearing is "the art of hearing" for ministers. Until you have learnt to listen repetitively, you have not learnt to listen.

God will always speak once but you must hear it at least twice. Indeed, there are messages you need to hear a hundred times over. Many people are poor listeners. "Poor listening leads to assumptions and misunderstandings."

There may be one thousand people in a church service but perhaps only one or two will listen to the message twice. Those are the people that are called by God. Without listening to a message several times over, you will not benefit from it.

Many years ago, I discovered a message by Kenneth Hagin entitled "The Greater One In You." I listened to this particular message hundreds of times. Getting to the end of this message, Kenneth Hagin would burst out in tongues and speak in tongues intermittently for about thirty minutes. I just enjoyed listening to this message over and over. I enjoyed listening to the tongues. I felt encouraged when I listened to the message. I felt empowered and emboldened for ministry.

I never attended Kenneth Hagin's Bible school but as I listened to that message, I realised that he was preaching to his Bible school students. By listening to this message over and over, I became a Bible student without intending to. I enjoyed the Bible school environment without even knowing that I was participating in a Bible school class. Even up till today, I benefit from that message.

The reality is that we do not retain much of what we hear. Many different secular studies show that we need to listen more than once. You must rise up with zeal and become an ardent repetitive listener to messages. As you will see from the following secular studies, it is important to hear something many times over before it has an impact on your life.

The Law of Exposure

Some people say repeating a message three times is enough, whilst some believe in the rule of listening seven times. There was a study from a large American firm investigating the optimum number of exposures required for audio messages. They concluded that between six to twenty times was best.

The Law of Seven

Perhaps the rule of seven from the world of marketing will throw light on how many times you need to listen to a message. The rule of seven states that a prospect needs to hear the advertiser's message at least seven times before they will take action to buy that product or service.

The Law of Retention

We retain approximately ten per cent of what we see, thirty to forty per cent of what we see and hear and ninety percent of what we see, hear and do.

The Law of Remembrance

People remember ten per cent of what they read, twenty per cent of what they hear, thirty per cent of what they see.

Decide to become a good repetitive listener! Be a serial hearer! Open yourself to the word of God. Listen to a message between six and twenty times. Remember the rule of seven. It takes seven exposures before anyone is convinced about something. Keep exposing yourself to the word of God. Keep exposing yourself to the videos. You are exposing yourself to the right things. There is going to be a major change in your life through repetitive listening.

CHAPTER 15

Seeing and Hearing Never Ends

All things are full of labour; man cannot utter it: THE EYE IS NOT SATISFIED WITH SEEING, NOR THE EAR FILLED WITH HEARING.

Ecclesiastes 1:8

Hearing is forever! Hearing will never end in your life. Hearing continues endlessly throughout your life. There is no minister who can say he has matured out of the art of hearing.

The ear is not filled with hearing. There are those who feel they know so much that they need not listen to preaching and teaching. Some older ministers of the gospel do not watch any videos or listen to messages. They feel that they have graduated from the need to hear and to see.

Our walk with the Lord never ends and until we are safely in glory, we will need to be listening, hearing, noticing, watching, learning and receiving. All through my life, I have had various experiences as I gave myself to seeing and hearing.

In 1979, I discovered Kenneth Hagin, a great prophet of God. Someone introduced me to his books and tapes. As I began listening to this man of God, I noticed a change in my life.

I was a Scripture Union leader and I had the duty of preaching to my little congregation of students. I noticed that when I preached the same message that Kenneth Hagin preached, there was an amazing impact. Everyone was impacted and made comments about the amazing teaching I had delivered. I did not tell anyone I had listened to a Kenneth Hagin tape. But I definitely noticed the parallel. But that was not all. I was going to have another experience ten years later, as I continued listening.

In 1988, whilst in medical school I had another experience that changed my life. I was listening to Kenneth Hagin preaching. I was praying and waiting on God in a town in Ghana. In the middle of the night, something happened to me. Something jumped out of the tape and entered into my belly. I heard a voice that said, "From today you can teach." That was the beginning of my teaching ministry.

And the spirit entered into me when he spake unto me, and set me upon my feet, that I heard him that spake unto me.

Ezekiel 2:2

Somewhere in 1994, whilst at home waiting on God, I was listening to a man of God who was preaching on television. He was teaching the word of God and would pray for the sick after his long sessions of teaching. One afternoon whilst I was lying down in my study, I suddenly began to understand the long-winded and mysterious teaching of this man of God. I was not watching the television. I was lying on my face and praying. I was hearing and occasionally I would get up to see. Suddenly, I began to receive and understand. Scripture teaches that the Holy Spirit works by bringing things to our minds.

But the Comforter, which is the Holy Ghost, whom the Father will send in my name, he shall teach you all things, and BRING ALL THINGS TO YOUR REMEMBRANCE, whatsoever I have said unto you.

John 14:26

When the anointing is flowing, new understanding and new truths come alive to you. The scripture is so clear on this. New truths came alive to me that afternoon and I entered into the healing ministry. When the Spirit is come, He guides you into truths.

Howbeit WHEN HE, THE SPIRIT OF TRUTH, IS COME, HE WILL GUIDE YOU INTO ALL TRUTH: for he shall not speak of himself; but whatsoever he shall hear, that shall he speak: and he will shew you things to come.

John 16:13

Somewhere in 1999, I was waiting on the Lord. I was fasting and praying and playing videos of miracle services. It was a very intense atmosphere and I felt the Lord telling me, "I have given you a healing ministry." I can still see myself fasting, lying down and dehydrated as I came to the end of that fast. I had no idea what those words about my healing ministry would mean. I never knew that one day someone would call me a "magician" because of the miracles in my ministry.

In 2014, I was praying in the middle of the night and listening to a message from a man of God. He was teaching a powerful message to thousands of people. Suddenly, at 2.00am, I jumped up as the truth and the teaching rocked my soul and my spirit. I could not help myself as I began to leap and jump in the dark. I knew I had found important teaching for my life and ministry. When the anointing is flowing, teachings flow to you.

But the anointing which ye have received of him abideth in you, and ye need not that any man teach you: but as the same anointing teacheth you of all things, and is truth, and is no lie, and even as it hath taught you, ye shall abide in him.

1 John 2:27

I had received something that changed my whole ministry yet again. There is no end to seeing and hearing because the ear is never filled. I am always expecting a special charging up when I give myself to seeing and hearing.

CHAPTER 16

Seeing and Hearing Must be with Faith

Let us therefore fear, lest, a promise being left us of entering into his rest, any of you should seem to come short of it. FOR UNTO US WAS THE GOSPEL PREACHED, AS WELL AS UNTO THEM: BUT THE WORD PREACHED DID NOT PROFIT THEM, NOT BEING MIXED WITH FAITH IN THEM THAT HEARD IT.

Hebrews 4:1-2

Why is it that some people are blessed when they hear and others are not so blessed? What is the difference? Notice the scripture: "For unto us was the gospel preached as well as unto them: but the word that was preached did not profit them."

Hearing properly is to hear with faith. Judas was sitting at the table when Jesus said, "One of you will betray me." Other disciples were concerned as to who the betrayer was.

Hearing properly is to hear with faith. Judas Iscariot did not hear with faith.

And truly the Son of man goeth, as it was determined: but woe unto that man by whom he is betrayed! And they began to enquire among themselves, which of them it was that should do this thing.

Luke 22:22-23

Judas listened to this message. Jesus revealed that He knew all about Judas' wicked behaviour. Yet, the message did not benefit him because he did not hear with faith.

One day, I had the same experience. I preached a message in which I spoke about Judas. A Judas was sitting right there. This Judas did not budge an inch. I gave examples that fitted the exact description of the Judas who was sitting right there. The Judas did not flinch. Judas never said anything. Judas never sought to see me and make amends. Judas thought I had no idea about all that he was up to. How amazing it is when people hear a message without faith. It simply does not benefit them. This Judas continued in his accursed path to his own destruction.

When you listen to preaching, you must mix it with faith. You must have faith when you hear the word of God and believe that it applies to you. Indeed, as I preached about Judas, several other people who had no semblance or connection to any spirit of Judas spoke to me in deep concern for their souls. They were very worried, thinking that perhaps a spirit of Judas could affect them.

I smiled to and said to myself as they spoke, "The real Judas has not noticed that the preaching concerns him." Notice how the disciples were concerned about who the Judas could be. Peter went as far as to find out from the Lord about who exactly Judas was. Judas did not bother to find out who "Judas" was. He heard what Jesus said but did not mix it with faith.

> When Jesus had thus said, he was troubled in spirit, and testified, and said, Verily, verily, I say unto you, that one of you shall betray me. Then the disciples looked one on another, doubting of whom he spake. Now there was leaning on Jesus' bosom one of his disciples, whom Jesus loved. Simon Peter therefore beckoned to him, that he should ask who it should be of whom he spake. He then lying on Jesus' breast saith unto him, Lord, who is it? Jesus answered, HE IT IS, TO WHOM I SHALL GIVE A SOP, WHEN I HAVE DIPPED IT. AND WHEN HE HAD DIPPED THE SOP, HE GAVE IT TO JUDAS ISCARIOT, THE SON OF SIMON. After the sop Satan entered into him. Then said Jesus unto him, That thou doest, do quickly.
>
> John 13:21-27

Today, when you hear the word of God, do not be hard or stubborn. Always believe that every message, good or bad, applies to you.

> **While it is said, To day if ye will hear his voice, HARDEN NOT YOUR HEARTS, as in the provocation. For some, when they had heard, did provoke: howbeit not all that came out of Egypt by Moses.**
> **Hebrews 3:15-16**

Hearing must be without stubbornness. Hearing must be without the hardening of the heart. You are unable to receive a message when your heart is hardened. When you harden your heart, the message bounces off you. When Peter heard that there was a Judas, the message did not bounce off his heart. He considered it deeply and wanted to be sure that it was not him.

A hardened heart is revealed when a person shows no emotion. A hardened heart shows no concern and shows no feelings. A hardened heart is revealed when a person receives strong repeated messages but does not change.

When you listen to a particular preacher for some time, you can develop a hardening of heart towards the messages. A voice within you will tell you, "I know what it is about."

Another voice will tell you, "It is the same thing as the last time." Another voice will tell you, "I know this message very well." All these thoughts harden your heart and you are unable to receive.

You need to switch quickly and listen to other things so that you can come back with a softened attitude and heart. Sometimes when you listen to other preaching you appreciate the teaching that God has for you.

CHAPTER 17

Seeing and Hearing Guarantees No Loss of the Anointing

THEREFORE WE OUGHT TO GIVE THE MORE EARNEST HEED TO THE THINGS WHICH WE HAVE HEARD, LEST AT ANY TIME WE SHOULD LET THEM SLIP. For if the word spoken by angels was stedfast, and every transgression and disobedience received a just recompence of reward.

Hebrews 2:1-2

Hearing again and again ensures that you do not lose sections of your gifts and callings. Letting things slip is to lose them. Things heard tend to slip. That is why we need to hear and hear again and again.

When you develop the art of seeing and hearing, you will find out that things that you have heard tend to get lost. Many people ask, "How do you maintain your zeal?" "How have you been able to stay serving the Lord in the same way for so many years?"

Most definitely you will find that things you believe will begin to slip and you will begin to lose them. This is why you need to keep listening to the same things over and over again.

One day I was having a prayer time. I was soaking in messages from Kenneth Hagin. Suddenly I came across the same message that I had listened to twenty-five years earlier when the power of God came upon me. As I listened to this message, I became transfixed and overawed at the power of God that was still flowing from that message to me.

Because I had not listened to this message for some time, some of the message, the power and the awesome anointing was beginning to slip. God was restoring me to that same level of power.

CHAPTER 18

Seeing and Hearing Guarantees a Foundation for Your Ministry

That which was from the beginning, WHICH WE HAVE HEARD, WHICH WE HAVE SEEN WITH OUR EYES, which we have looked upon, and our hands have handled, of the Word of life; ...That which we have seen and heard declare we unto you, that ye also may have fellowship with us: and truly our fellowship is with the Father, and with his Son Jesus Christ.

1 John 1:1, 3

What you will ever be able to declare, and what you will be able to minister will depend on the things you have seen and heard!

Your whole ministry depends on what you have seen and heard before. You can never do things that you have not seen. You need to see certain things in order to experience them. John experienced certain things and heard certain things. That was the foundation for his ministry.

What you will ever be able to declare, and what you will be able to minister will depend on the things you have seen and heard.

Without seeing, it will be impossible to comprehend that something is possible. As the years go by, I realise that I am able to do only the things that I have seen and heard.

I am able to have a mega church because I have seen a mega church in action. For twenty-five years I have been travelling to Korea, where the largest church was based. Why did I go to Korea in 1994? To see a mega church for myself! On the first Sunday I visited Korea, I attended all seven services that were held. It did not matter to me that the services were being held in the Korean language and I could not understand anything. I was happy to see that seven services could be held on a Sunday in the same building.

I saw that the pastors, the church members lingered around the church till the evening. In Korea, I saw church offices that were active and real. I saw pastors' offices. I saw church members coming for counselling in droves. I saw lady pastors. I saw many smaller churches within the one big church. I saw thousands of people attending church. I saw a strong pastor leading his congregation.

I saw a church growing from a tent into a huge cathedral. I saw branches of the church. I saw a pastor who had taken church growth to its logical and extreme conclusion. I saw full time ministry. I visited offices. I saw elders having meetings.

I saw businessmen having meetings in the church on Sunday afternoons. I saw corridors and offices filled with charts, maps, pictures and data. I met cheerful people who were happy to be in church for long hours. I met church secretaries who were manning offices and answering questions. I saw church bookshops which had books, pictures, souvenirs and many other things which would keep you in there for hours. I saw multiple services. I saw pastors keeping to time. I saw the changeover of church services.

I saw board meetings. I saw a television ministry and a television studio. I saw the media ministry of a church which worked behind the scenes. I saw the neat dressing and uniforms of the ushers. I saw multiple choirs, each with a different uniform and different set of musicians. I saw several amazing choir conductors, conducting their choirs. I saw how they hosted international guests. I saw how to receive a guest and how to treat them. I saw the kind of hotel to put international guests in. I saw how to decorate church offices. I saw multiple sets of instruments, multiple pulpits, fridges, kitchens, halls, seats and equipment everywhere.

I saw a mega church and I realised that what was written in the books could become a reality. I saw how a poor church could become a rich church. I saw how a poor area of the city could be turned into a nice area.

Indeed, what you have seen and what you have heard is the foundation of your entire ministry. *If you have not seen it, you are not likely to be able to do it.* This is the reason why we travel to places. We travel so that we can see and receive. Seeing and hearing is the most important activity for a minister. You must see many things. You must receive many things. You will receive all these things by seeing and hearing. Seeing and hearing is the foundation for your ministry.

Today, I am experiencing a healing ministry. I have seen miracles in every country and crusade I have conducted. One day, I had a crusade in the northern part of Ghana. I preached the word of God and there were miracles and healings. After the crusade, an elderly pastor came to see me. He said, "I think I should tell you something."

He continued, "Do not assume that everyone who prays for the sick will see healings and miracles."

Then he told me, "I was in this town when an evangelist held a crusade here in the very same spot you are holding your crusade. This evangelist advertised miracles and healings. Unfortunately, when the evangelist prayed for the sick no one was healed."

The pastor said to me, "Because there were no miracles, the crowd became agitated and began to hoot at the evangelist and to stone him."

He continued, "I think you should value the great miracle and healing ministry that you are experiencing. Do not take it for granted. It is a great blessing. Not everyone has it that way."

I was really touched by this testimony and I began to value the miracle and healing ministry that I was experiencing. How did it all begin? It started by seeing and hearing! Many years ago, a great evangelist called T. L. Osborn visited Ghana. He held his crusade at the Independence Square of the nation. I was a student then but I attended the crusade.

At T.L. Osborn's crusade in Accra, my soul was deeply affected. I saw the crowds at the Independence Square in Accra and I saw people being healed for the first time in my life. I had never seen anything like that before. During the miracle time, I moved to the back of the stage and I met a woman with a huge goitre. She wanted me to pray for her. Perhaps, she thought I was part of the American team that had come with T. L. Osborn. As soon as I touched her, the huge swelling on her neck disappeared. I was shocked. Immediately, a queue formed in front of me. It was a queue of sick people who wanted me to pray for them.

That was the first miracle I saw in my life! I could not even believe that it was real. Seeing real miracles and hearing of them from the stage inspired me and affected my young soul.

Obviously, it gave me a taste for open-air crusades. It gave me an appetite for miracles. I had now seen and heard an international open-air campaign by an international evangelist.

You cannot minister what you have not seen or heard. John made it clear, "That which we have seen and that which we have heard is what we are ministering to you." You can only minister what you have seen and heard.

That is why you must travel and see! You must not only travel when you are invited to preach. You must travel to see, experience and feel different things. It is very unlikely that you will do things that you have not seen before. Do not be too proud to travel and sit in places, just to imbibe the atmosphere. Do not think you know everything. There are things you have not yet seen.

CHAPTER 19

Seeing and Hearing Confirms Your New Level

I have heard of thee by the hearing of the ear: BUT NOW MINE EYE SEETH THEE.

Job 42:5

T hank God for the grace of hearing. But when your eye begins to see the great things that you have heard of, you will enter your new level.

Enter higher dimensions of ministry by combining seeing with hearing. Seeing takes you into a higher dimension of what God has given you through hearing. Seeing is your master key to entering the next level.

Today, I want you to understand that seeing takes you higher. Seeing does something that hearing does not do. "...But now mine eye seeth thee"!

This is why I flew to Tulsa, Oklahoma to see Kenneth Hagin before he died.

I had heard him preaching all my life. But now my eye was seeing him. I sat in the church building as Kenneth Hagin preached. My eyes were fixed on him. I was full of wonder and amazement as I looked on this man who had had these visions of Jesus. Walking in that campus and breathing the air was like breathing the air of heaven to me. I felt I was receiving something at every moment.

On one of the days, the ushers wanted to take me upstairs. I asked the usher where he came from. He said he was from an eastern European country. I told him I had come from very far away in Africa and there was no way I could go upstairs. I needed to be near the front. I needed to see everything there was to see. I needed to attend everything I could attend and touch everything I could touch. It is true that my ear had been hearing. But now I was shooting to another level by what I was seeing. Oh, how I loved those moments; being present in a miraculous and anointed place!

I bought every tape and book I could lay my hands on. I bought everything there was to buy. I was happy to be there in a place where Kenneth Hagin himself was.

I saw a pastors' conference. I experienced a conference that was dedicated to ministry. Everything that was preached was important to ministry.

I saw the Bible school. I saw the lecture halls. I met students. I went to visit the Dean of the school and interviewed him. I asked him what problems they had. I saw the curriculum of the school. I saw the healing school. I saw Kenneth Hagin's car parked in front of the church. I saw the neatness and the order in which the whole campus was run. As I saw many things, my heart was filled with desire and passion to go back to Ghana to do the same.

Outside the main hall, I explored every nook and cranny that I could gain access to without being stopped. I wanted to see everything and I wanted to know everything. I saw the car parks everywhere, all around the school. I roamed around outside and crossed a little river to a section dedicated to alumni of the school. I looked across the streets and saw the accommodation and the housing units that had been acquired for the students. My ears had heard but now my eyes had seen it all.

On one occasion, the Holy Spirit prompted my heart to sow a seed in Kenneth Hagin's life. I was invited to the back of the stage, where the board members were fellowshipping. Within a few seconds, my eye and my heart had taken it all in. God had made me to see many things which few people had seen. Your whole ministry is based on what you have seen.

Today, we have a similar serene campus with many students from all over the world. I am experiencing what I saw. My ears had heard Kenneth Hagin preaching but now my eyes had seen it all. I saw what was involved in holding pastors' conferences, publishing millions of books, building a campus and running a Bible school.

Seeing guarantees your new level in ministry. I am experiencing a higher level on ministry and it is based on what I have seen and not just what I have heard.

CHAPTER 20

Seeing and Hearing Impacts Your Soul

And turning the cities of Sodom and Gomorrha into ashes condemned them with an overthrow, making them an ensample unto those that after should live ungodly; And delivered just Lot, vexed with the filthy conversation of the wicked: (For that righteous man dwelling among them, in SEEING AND HEARING, VEXED HIS RIGHTEOUS SOUL FROM DAY TO DAY WITH THEIR UNLAWFUL DEEDS;)

2 Peter 2:6-8

S eeing and hearing affects your soul. Seeing and hearing affects your emotions. Your soul consists of your will, your emotions and your feelings. Seeing and hearing affects your heart and your mind in a way that you will never understand.

Lot was affected negatively by the things he was seeing and hearing. This is because seeing and hearing always affects your soul. When you see an unemotional, cold, detached and inexpressive minister, it is because his soul is not in the ministry. Loving God must be done with all your heart, mind and soul. Serving God must be done with all your heart, with all your soul and with all your mind.

I attended funerals where the priests looked uninterested in what they were doing. They were completely detached from the ceremony and the families who were grieving. Many pastors stand in the pulpit but are not consumed with their calling and ministry. I have seen church services where the priests preached uninspiring and dead messages. I was turned away from the church and my soul was affected. I hated religion and I think I could have become an atheist because of the dead religion that I found in churches.

Seeing and hearing is like experiencing something in real life. The more you see and the more you hear, the more real it becomes to you. The more you watch videos of church services and miracle healings, the more it feels like you are actually doing it even though you have never done it before. Seeing and hearing is the highest form of training you can give yourself.

One day, a young man was getting married to a beautiful lady. They sat before me and discussed their visions and dreams for their honeymoon and marriage. We laughed happily together. Then it came out that the young man was a virgin but the lady was not. She was experienced with sex but he had never had sex before. I asked him whether he felt intimidated by the fact that he was a novice and that his bride was well experienced with different men.

He laughed and said, "Not at all. I am not intimidated at all."

"Oh, I see. How come you are not intimidated," I asked.

He said, "I have watched a lot of pornography. To me, it is like the real thing. I am not intimidated at all. I think I will rather be teaching her what to do."

I realised how much seeing and hearing can impact your soul. If seeing and hearing can make a virgin feel that he is not a virgin, then "seeing and hearing" is a powerful tool.

You must use this powerful tool of seeing and hearing for good. Use it to become a powerful minister. Learn how to do everything in the ministry. When you have a few moments with a great leader, watch what he does. Learn how to lead by watching a great leader!

CHAPTER 21

Seeing and Hearing Guarantees You Become a Good Teacher

Thou therefore, my son, be strong in the grace that is in Christ Jesus. AND THE THINGS THAT THOU HAST HEARD OF ME AMONG MANY WITNESSES, THE SAME COMMIT THOU TO FAITHFUL MEN, WHO SHALL BE ABLE TO TEACH OTHERS ALSO.

2 Timothy 2:1-2

Paul taught Timothy how to become a great teacher. He told him to listen and to teach the things he had heard. What you hear is the basis of your teaching ministry. The hallmark of your ministry is what you teach and preach.

I have never seen a great minister who does not have a good message. You can become a preacher or a teacher by deciding to teach what you have heard. Seeing and hearing, therefore, becomes the foundation of your teaching ministry.

Do not be shy to learn how to preach by copying other preachers. This scripture is telling us directly that we should copy the teachings of our teachers. It is telling us to teach the same teachings that our teachers taught.

Many years ago, I discovered this secret: listen to your teachers so much till you can teach exactly what they taught. Indeed, listen to them so much that you can preach their message better than they preach it.

I do not have any original message. Everything I preach has come from listening to others. I have a list of people whose messages have given me the content of what to preach. I am always searching for new and exciting messages that will give me something to preach. I am amazed at those who want to be "original".

Your whole ministry depends on what you teach and preach. Jesus sent people to preach and to teach the word of God. Jesus sent people with a specific message. All through the Bible, God sent His servants to repeat the messages that He had given to others.

Jesus preached what He learnt from Isaiah. He preached exactly the same words as Isaiah. As a result, when we are quoting those scriptures we either quote from the Old Testament or the New Testament because it is the same thing.

The Spirit of the Lord God is upon me; because the Lord hath anointed me to preach good tidings unto the meek; he hath sent me to bind up the brokenhearted, to proclaim liberty to the captives, and the opening of the prison to them that are bound; To proclaim the acceptable year of the Lord, and the day of vengeance of our God; to comfort all that mourn;

Isaiah 61:1-2

The Spirit of the Lord is upon me, because he hath anointed me to preach the gospel to the poor; he hath sent me to heal the brokenhearted, to preach deliverance to the captives, and recovering of sight to the blind, to set at liberty them that are bruised, To preach the acceptable year of the Lord.

Luke 4:18-19

John the Baptist preached what he learnt from Isaiah. He preached exactly the same words as Isaiah. When we are quoting those scriptures we either quote from the Old Testament or the New Testament because it is almost exactly the same thing.

The voice of him that crieth in the wilderness, Prepare ye the way of the Lord, make straight in the desert a highway for our God. Every valley shall be exalted, and every mountain and hill shall be made low: and the crooked shall be made straight, and the rough places plain: and the glory of the Lord shall be revealed, and all flesh shall see it together: for the mouth of the Lord hath spoken it.

Isaiah 40:3-5

As it is written in the book of the words of Esaias the prophet, saying, The voice of one crying in the wilderness, Prepare ye the way of the Lord, make his paths straight. Every valley shall be filled, and every mountain and hill shall be brought low; and the crooked shall be made straight, and the rough ways shall be made smooth; And all flesh shall see the salvation of God.

Luke 3:4-6

Peter, the apostle, preached what he learnt from the prophet Joel. As a result, we either quote from the Old Testament or the New Testament when we went to refer to it.

And it shall come to pass afterward, that I will pour out my spirit upon all flesh; and your sons and your daughters shall prophesy, your old men shall dream dreams, your young men shall see visions: And also upon the servants and upon the handmaids in those days will I pour out my spirit. And I will shew wonders in the heavens and in the earth, blood, and fire, and pillars of smoke. The sun shall be turned into darkness, and the moon into blood, before the great and the terrible day of the Lord come. And it shall come to pass, that whosoever shall call on the name of the Lord shall be delivered: for in mount Zion and in Jerusalem shall be deliverance, as the Lord hath said, and in the remnant whom the Lord shall call.

Joel 2:28-32

But this is that which was spoken by the prophet Joel; and it shall come to pass in the last days, saith God, I will pour out of my Spirit upon all flesh: and your sons and your daughters shall prophesy, and your young men shall see visions, and your old men shall dream dreams: and on my servants and on my handmaidens I will pour out in those days of my Spirit; and they shall prophesy: and I will shew wonders in heaven above, and signs in the earth beneath; blood, and fire, and vapour of smoke: The sun shall be turned into darkness, and the moon into blood, before that great and notable day of the Lord come: and it shall come to pass, that whosoever shall call on the name of the Lord shall be saved.

Acts 2:16-21

If such great people preached exactly the same thing as their fathers, why do you have a problem preaching the same thing that someone else has preached?

CHAPTER 22

Seeing and Hearing Guarantees Your Rise into Honour and Glory

FOR HE RECEIVED FROM GOD THE FATHER HONOUR AND GLORY, WHEN THERE CAME SUCH A VOICE to him FROM THE EXCELLENT GLORY, this is my beloved Son, in whom I am well pleased. And this voice which came from heaven we heard, when we were with him in the holy mount.

2 Peter 1:17-18

There is a place called the "excellent glory". From that excellent glory, you will receive glory for your ministry.

Glory and honour will come to you from the excellent glory when you hear certain things.

There is a voice that will guarantee your rise into honour and glory in the ministry.

Enter the glorious anointed realm of ministry by hearing and hearing and hearing.

Glory and honour is what Jesus received when the voice came to Him. Glory means beauty. Honour means respect and reverence. God will give you beauty, respect and reverence. Your ministry will receive glory and honour through a voice.

Which voice has God chosen to bless your life? I received honour and glory into my ministry when such a voice came to me from the excellent glory. In my little room in Suhum, Ghana, a voice came to me from the Lord. The voice said "From today you can teach." I received the glory of my teaching ministry. The beauty of my teaching ministry came to me that night. The beauty and the glory of the messages I preach came to me that night. The beauty and the glory of being able to captivate audiences for hours on end with teachings from the word of God came to me that night.

The beauty and glory of an international ministry came to me the night I heard that voice. The beauty and glory of being listened to by different people all over the world came to me when I heard the voice. God brings glory to your life from the excellent glory. The glory of my books being read and being sought after by many people came to me from the excellent glory. Today, God will send glory into your ministry!

One day, I passed by a church that was located in an old part of the city of Accra. It was situated near where I started my ministry. This church was meeting in a small-dilapidated building made up of left-over wooden construction boards. The name of this church was similar to the original name of our church. The

Holy Spirit whispered to me, "I could have left you in this state. You would have been right here, never rising out of the ground. Many people have started churches but their ministries never become glorious or honourable. Many churches began at the same time that your church began."

What you need is the glory and the honour from the excellent glory.

Jesus received the most glorious and honourable ministry of all. Today, we all honour Jesus Christ.

Today, we all read His words. His words are the most beautiful words ever spoken. His words have been translated into every conceivable language. Jesus never travelled more than two hundred miles from His birthplace. Yet His ministry has spread to every nook and cranny of this globe. Jesus Christ never wrote a book and yet more books have been written about Him than anyone else. The books about His life, the Gospels, have been produced and re-produced more than any other manuscript in the world. What a glorious and honourable ministry Jesus received.

Today, the mention of the name of Jesus is like music in the ears of millions of people. It has been two thousand years since Jesus left the scene; but His ministry is so glorious and so honourable that it continues to persist. Most ministries die after the first generation. We cannot say that about Jesus. We cannot count the number of generations through which His ministry has lasted. Today, many songs are composed about Jesus: [1]*"How sweet the name of Jesus sounds!"* [2]*"How I love Jesus."* [3]*"Jesus is the answer!"* [4]*"Jesu, joy of man's desiring."* [5]*"Jesus, Saviour of the world!"*

Has any song been composed about you? Do you ever receive such honour? Indeed, God wants to pass some honour and glory to you from the excellent glory. Open yourself to the mystery of seeing and hearing. Seeing and hearing is the master key to receiving beauty from the excellent glory.

---

1. John Newton   2. Reba McEntire   3. Andraé Crouch   4.Johann Sebastian Bach 5. First Love Music

74

CHAPTER 23

Seeing and Hearing Guarantees You Are Becoming a Learned Person

The Lord God hath given me the tongue of the learned, that I should know how to speak a word in season to him that is weary: HE WAKENETH MORNING BY MORNING, HE WAKENETH MINE EAR TO HEAR AS THE LEARNED. The Lord God hath opened mine ear, and I was not rebellious, neither turned away back.

Isaiah 50:4-5

Become a learned minister! Become someone who knows more than the people he is leading. People follow someone who knows a little more than they do. Become a learned person by soaking in messages! Seeing and hearing is your master key to becoming a learned minister.

One of the most important subjects is history. History is important because life goes round in cycles. What happened yesterday is what is going to happen tomorrow.

> The thing that hath been, it is that which shall be; and that which is done is that which shall be done: and there is no new thing under the sun. Is there any thing whereof it may be said, See, this is new? it hath been already of old time, which was before us.
>
> Ecclesiastes 1:9-10

Many of us did not study history in school. And even if we had, we would not remember much of it. Most of the history students I know are unable to apply what they learnt in school to their real lives. You can overcome your history handicap by seeing and hearing. Watch and learn what happened in the past. God will speak to you prophetically when you study history.

Many prophecies are declarations that that which has been is that which shall be. Spend time watching videos and documentaries that teach you things that you do not know.

Become a master of science, history, economics, finance, management, psychology, philosophy and sociology by the art of seeing and hearing!

CHAPTER 24

Seeing and Hearing Guarantees Your Journey into the Supernatural Anointing

Now it came to pass in the thirtieth year, in the fourth month, in the fifth day of the month, AS I WAS AMONG THE CAPTIVES BY THE RIVER OF CHEBAR, that the heavens were opened, and I saw visions of God. In the fifth day of the month, which was the fifth year of king Jehoiachin's captivity, The word of the LORD came expressly unto Ezekiel the priest, the son of Buzi, in the land of the Chaldeans by the river Chebar; and the hand of the Lord was there upon him.

Ezekiel 1:1-3

1. ***Seeing and hearing is part of the supernatural journey.*** Seeing and hearing leads you into higher realms of the supernatural. It leads you to the anointing. Ezekiel entered the supernatural realm when he both saw and heard from the realm of God.

Your eyes must see and your ears must hear if you are to move above the ordinary Christian laity and experience supernatural things. Almost every supernatural experience of my life has come through seeing and hearing.

2. ***Falling down is part of the supernatural journey.***

As the appearance of the bow that is in the cloud in the day of rain, so was the appearance of the brightness round about. This was the appearance of the likeness of the glory of the Lord. AND WHEN I SAW IT, I FELL UPON MY FACE, AND I HEARD A VOICE OF ONE THAT SPAKE.

Ezekiel 1:28

What are you seeing and what are you hearing? Look at Ezekiel's journey into the supernatural. He fell on his face when he saw supernatural things. The supernatural experience made Ezekiel fall on his face. There are times I have had to lie down in the presence of the Lord, unable to move. Even though the supernatural is the spirit world, it has an effect on you physically.

3. ***Standing up is part of the supernatural journey.***

And he said unto me, Son of man, stand upon thy feet, and I will speak unto thee. And the spirit entered into me when he spake unto me, and set me upon my feet, that I heard him that spake unto me.

Ezekiel 2:1-2

Whilst Ezekiel was down on his face, he had yet another supernatural experience. God told him to stand up. The anointing was about to enter into Ezekiel as he stood up. There are times

I have had to stand up in the presence of the Lord. This is what happened to me some years ago when I was listening to Kenneth Hagin's preaching in a town called Suhum. The Spirit entered into me as I was listening to Kenneth Hagin preach. I felt the power of God coming into me and I heard a voice saying, "From today you can teach."

4. The Spirit entering into you is part of the supernatural journey.

While Peter yet spake these words, the Holy Ghost fell on all them which heard the word.

Acts 10:44

The Holy Spirit entered into Ezekiel when the Lord spoke to him. The anointing of the Holy Spirit was now in Ezekiel. This is what happened when Peter preached in Cornelius' house. As Peter preached the word of God, the anointing fell on the people. The Holy Spirit came upon the whole congregation and they began to speak in tongues. Without the anointing you cannot do very much. God will use you mightily when the anointing is on you!

5. The Spirit entering you again and again is part of the spiritual journey.

I have felt the Holy Spirit entering into me again and again. At different places and at different times, the Spirit has come into me. Each time the Holy Spirit enters you; you may not have the exact same experience.

The first time when the Spirit entered into Ezekiel, he was by the river Chebar. The second time when the Holy Spirit entered into him, he was in the plain. Ezekiel was told to go to the plain and there he would hear from God. It was a slightly different experience and he reported it a little differently. The Holy Spirit enters you again and again as you yield yourself to Him.

Sometimes God needs you to go to certain places in order for Him to speak to you. Why did God not allow Ezekiel to stay by the river Chebar, but wanted him to go to the plain? Without going to certain places you are not likely to hear from God.

And the hand of the Lord was there upon me; and he said unto me, ARISE, GO FORTH INTO THE PLAIN, and I will there talk with thee. Then I arose, and went forth into the plain: and, behold, the glory of the Lord stood there, as the glory which I saw by the river of Chebar: and I fell on my face. Then the spirit entered into me, and set me upon my feet, and spake with me, and said unto me, Go, shut thyself within thine house.

Ezekiel 3:22-24

Ezekiel is one of the most mysterious Jewish prophets. He experienced amazing visions that have captivated Jews and Christians alike. You are about to have such amazing experiences. You will receive the anointing of the Holy Spirit as you listen to the Word and go to the places God wants you to go to.

CHAPTER 25

Seeing and Hearing Makes You Know What to Speak and Do

THOSE THINGS, WHICH YE HAVE BOTH LEARNED, AND RECEIVED, AND HEARD, AND SEEN IN ME, DO: and the God of peace shall be with you.

Philippians 4:9

For we cannot but SPEAK THE THINGS WHICH WE HAVE SEEN AND HEARD.

Acts 4:20

What is going to be your next step in ministry? What does God want you to do? Your next step in ministry is going to come from what you have seen and heard.

You will only do the things that you have seen and heard. If you have not seen it, you cannot do it. If you have not heard it, you cannot speak about it.

How do you know what to do in ministry? The Holy Spirit will lead you. And He will lead you by the mystery of seeing and hearing. What you see and hear is directly connected to what you must do.

One day I was invited to minister in a church in South Africa. This church was expanding rapidly and they were expecting a large overflow. They fixed a tent outside the church to seat all the extra people who were expected for this programme. The programme was a great success and there were people sitting in the tent every night.

The next year, I was invited to the church to help raise funds and launch the building of a new cathedral. This programme was actually held in a tent. For the first time, I preached in a tent and raised funds in a tent. Later that year I was musing over an instruction that the Holy Spirit had given me to begin having crusades. I was just wondering how to begin these crusades. Then I remembered the tent in which I had preached and I suddenly knew what to do. Notice the scripture: Those things which you have both learned and received and heard and seen, DO!

God expects you to do the things He has allowed you to learn, to receive and to hear. The reason why you are clueless on what to do in ministry is because you have not seen and heard enough. The more things you see, the more you know and the more the Holy Spirit can guide you.

One day, I visited a church that had an assistant pastor who was rebellious. As I visited that church more often, I got to know that there were even more rebellious people sitting everywhere in the congregation. Then one day, I heard the news that this particular rebellious pastor had died. The senior pastor told me later, "All the rebellious pastors in my church are dead." He listed them and told me how each one of them had died. He never rebuked them. He never changed their positions. He never transferred them. They just died! Wow! I realised that was another way of dealing with rebellion: *leaving them to the hand of God.* God was showing me a way to deal with rebellion.

Notice again the scripture: Those things which you have both learned and received and heard and seen, DO! God always expects you to do what He has shown you.

CHAPTER 26

Seeing and Hearing Guarantees that You Know His Will

Came unto me, and stood, and said unto me, Brother Saul, receive thy sight. And the same hour I looked up upon him. And he said, The God of our fathers hath chosen thee, that THOU SHOULDEST KNOW HIS WILL, AND SEE THAT JUST ONE, AND SHOULDEST HEAR THE VOICE OF HIS MOUTH. For thou shalt be his witness unto all men of what thou hast seen and heard.

Acts 22:13-15

Knowing the will of God is critical to success in the ministry. God chose Paul so that he would see the Lord and hear the voice of His mouth. The combination of seeing and hearing was going to turn Paul into one of the most famous personalities of all time.

You need to stay on course throughout your ministry. You need to stay in the will of God. You will not only catch the anointing from listening to messages but you will find the will of God as you listen to preaching. What a blessing it is to have the mystery of seeing and hearing.

One day, I met a pastor who had been the assistant to a great man of God. Unfortunately, this great man of God had undergone various crises, including a divorce. The assistant pastor was happy to have lunch with me and tell me all the stories of his senior pastor's ministry. He began to describe what it was like to work with this man of God.

As I listened to this pastor, I realised that God wanted me to hear how the ministry of this great man of God was destroyed. The assistant pastor told me many details that were helpful guiding posts for me.

Seeing and Hearing Is the Key to Your Future Possessions

And the Lord said unto Abram, after that Lot was separated from him, Lift up now thine eyes, and LOOK FROM THE PLACE WHERE THOU ART NORTHWARD, AND SOUTHWARD, AND EASTWARD, AND WESTWARD: FOR ALL THE LAND WHICH THOU SEEST, TO THEE WILL I GIVE IT, and to thy seed for ever. And I will make thy seed as the dust of the earth: so that if a man can number the dust of the earth, then shall thy seed also be numbered.
Arise, walk through the land in the length of it and in the breadth of it; for I will give it unto thee.

Genesis 13:14-17

Once you have been called by God, expect the Lord to do with you what He did with Abraham. He will take you out on a trip and show you wonderful and amazing distant lands. He is putting that vision into your heart. He is expecting you to dream about it, imagine it and work towards it.

Abraham was asked to look towards the Promised Land. God wanted him to see it and desire it. You cannot desire something you have not seen before.

Seeing and hearing is your master key to what you will possess in the ministry. God is showing you a type of Promised Land. Every conference you participate in will expose you to seeing and hearing the Promised Land.

I possessed the apostolic ministry through seeing and hearing. You will possess the apostolic ministry through seeing and hearing too! The apostolic ministry of your life is going to come as you see and hear. Your desire to have many churches will increase when you see someone doing it. I remember a pastor who had only one church. When he came to a conference I held, he saw that it was possible to have many churches. This is what God does for you through seeing and hearing. Every conference you attend is an opportunity to see the person God wants you to become.

One day I took several pastors from Ghana to Nigeria. We filled an entire bus and drove from Ghana to Nigeria. I wanted them to see the mega churches of Nigeria. I was so enthralled by the ministries of *The Redeemed Church of God* and *Winners' Chapel*. I wanted all my pastors and leaders to see what great things God could do. They needed to see how large and expansive a church could become.

I possessed the prophetic ministry through seeing and hearing. You will possess the prophetic ministry through seeing and hearing. I possessed the prophetic ministry by listening to prophetic ministers. God showed Kenneth Hagin to me. He was a prophet and a teacher. By seeing him, I could tell where God wanted me to go and what He wanted me to become. By seeing and hearing prophets and teachers, my ministry climbed from plain teaching into the prophet and teacher's ministry.

I possessed the teaching ministry through seeing and hearing. You will possess the teaching ministry through seeing and hearing. God introduced me to Fred Price. Fred Price taught the word of God powerfully to his church. I watched him over and over again. Watching Fred Price's church, *Crenshaw Christian Center (CCC)*, was God's way of showing me the Promised Land. I looked at the north, south, east and west of Fred Price's ministry and I knew where God was taking me to. When I started my church, I decided to call it KCC so that it would be as close to Fred Price's church as possible. Just like He did for Abraham, God had showed me the wide and expansive Promised Land of a teacher's ministry.

I possessed the pastoral ministry through seeing and hearing. You will possess the pastoral ministry through seeing and hearing. I possessed the ministry of a mega church by attending Yonggi Cho's conferences and seeing Yonggi Cho pastor his seven hundred thousand-member church.

At the Church Growth Conference, I saw many pastors who had huge churches. I saw that it was possible. I heard messages that showed me that it was possible. Like Abraham, God was showing me things that were possible, things that could be and things that could happen. If I had not seen Yonggi Cho, I would not have known what God wanted to accomplish in me.

I possessed the evangelistic ministry by seeing and hearing. You will possess the evangelistic ministry through seeing and hearing. One day, I was in Nigeria and I decided to drive to a crusade Reinhard Bonnke was holding in a nearby city. We drove for several miles just to see the stage, the lights, the equipment, the set-up, the camp and even the empty field. I have also attended several Reinhard Bonnke crusades over the years.

Seeing the crowds standing like trees in a forest was all that God was showing me. He wanted me to see the Promised Land.

If you do not pay the price to travel to see and to hear, you will never know what God has in store for you. This is a new day. God wants you to see and to hear so that you can become a great apostle, prophet, evangelist, pastor and teacher. Do not think of what it will cost for you to go to places so that you can see and hear. Think about what you will receive if you give yourself to seeing and hearing.

CHAPTER 28

Seeing and Hearing Commissions You Into a Writing Ministry

I WAS IN THE SPIRIT ON THE LORD'S DAY, AND HEARD BEHIND ME A GREAT VOICE, as of a trumpet, Saying, I am Alpha and Omega, the first and the last: and, WHAT THOU SEEST, WRITE IN A BOOK, and send it unto the seven churches which are in Asia; unto Ephesus, and unto Smyrna, and unto Pergamos, and unto Thyatira, and unto Sardis, and unto Philadelphia, and unto Laodicea. And I turned to see the voice that spake with me. And being turned, I saw seven golden candlesticks;

Revelation 1:10-12

J ohn the apostle was commissioned to write books. His books are amongst the famous and the most published books in the world. His ministry of writing to the world came about through the mystery of seeing and hearing. He heard a voice from heaven telling him to write books. The commission was clear, he was to write what he had seen.

You can only write what you have seen. If you have not seen certain things, your writings will be immature and empty theories.

Many people attempt to write books. But not everyone has been commissioned to write books. Perhaps, you should allow God to take you on a journey of seeing and hearing. The more you see and the more you hear, the more you will have to write.

Experience is a product of seeing and hearing. Experience is the foundation on which God commissions you to write books. You must be fruitful and you must obey the Lord. If God has called you to write books then do so! Just remember that John was commissioned into writing by seeing and hearing.

You will notice that in this book, I have shared things that I have seen and heard. I have shared things that I have experienced practically. Indeed, it is my personal experience of seeing and hearing that has showed me how important the mystery of seeing and hearing is.

May you go higher in the ministry through seeing and hearing all that God has for you!

Conclusion

You will see and hear many things! It is your destiny to be blessed with seeing and hearing. A change in your life and in your level takes place through this blessing of seeing and hearing!

And further, by these, my son, be admonished: of making many books there is no end; and much study is a weariness of the flesh!